ALWAYS FERRARI

ALWAYS FERRARI

The Live Performance Edition

Steve Matchett

Also by Steve Matchett

The Formula 1 Trilogy

Life in the Fast Lane

The Mechanic's Tale

The Chariot Makers

Short Stories

These Desired Things

Other Writings

Three Men in a Boat – The 130th Birthday Celebration

Breaking Bread with Ayrton Senna – The Live Performance Edition

Always Ferrari – The Live Performance Edition

The Mr. Goodman Stories – The Armistice Centenary Edition

Audiobook Narrations

Life in the Fast Lane

The Mechanic's Tale

The Chariot Makers

These Desired Things

Three Men in a Boat – The 130th Birthday Celebration

Breaking Bread with Ayrton Senna – The Live Performance Edition

Always Ferrari – The Live Performance Edition

ACKNOWLEDGEMENTS

Mela Chan

Matt Coapman

THANK YOU

ISBN-9781094658261

FIRST EDITION – FIRST IMPRESSION

CONTENTS

Dedication

Introduction

Always Ferrari

Part One

Part Two

Part Three

DEDICATION

To the eternal memory of

Nigel Stepney

A man who gave his life to Formula 1

INTRODUCTION

I'm sometimes asked why I tend to refer to Scuderia Ferrari as 'Maranello' rather than simply 'Ferrari'. After all, Maranello is merely the name of the town in northern Italy that plays host to that world famous two-story brick building in which automotive magic happens, but it is not the official name of Enzo's celebrated road car company, nor of his highly esteemed racing division. This is all patently true, of course, and I do not disagree. During my years working in the grand prix pit lanes of the world, however, my Formula 1 colleagues from both my own team of Benetton Formula Ltd., and many of our rivals would invariably refer to the mechanics and engineers dressed in their distinctive yellow and black uniforms as 'the men from Maranello'.

The name has a certain poetic ring to it, but for many of those who dwell within the F1 paddock the resonance of 'the men from Maranello' goes far beyond its pleasing alliterative cadence. In a very demonstrative way, Ferrari and Maranello are inseparable, inextricably bound together.

Should one hear news that the Mercedes Formula 1 team is relocating from Brackley to Birmingham; or Renault's grand prix team is planning a move from Enstone to Edinburgh; or McLaren from Woking to Wolverhampton, no one (at least, hardly anyone beyond the workers themselves) would bat an eyelid or care a fig. The actual physical location of any Formula 1 team's headquarters is, largely, entirely irrelevant to their supporters. There is but one singular exception to this particular observation: Ferrari.

Take just one step through the exit doors of every other Formula 1 team in existence, walk the highstreets of the towns located nearest to them, and you'll encounter all but no evidence whatsoever to suggest a Formula 1 team is located close by. Zero evidence, most likely. Now, try taking a similar stroll around the narrow avenues and squat squares of the tiny Italian town of Maranello. On my own trips there I have never walked into a single bar, café or restaurant whose walls aren't ablaze with Ferrari flags, posters and photographs. Maranello embraces Ferrari with an overt, fervent passion; the two names share a symbiotic relationship: Ferrari's road car production facility employs hundreds of local residents, while their racing division gives work to hundreds more. Maranello's hotels burst at the seams with Ferrari tourists from around the globe, all longing to see something of the famous old road car factory, along with Scuderia Ferrari's newly-built headquarters; perhaps to catch a fleeting glimpse of prototype test cars roaring around the Fiorano race track; to visit the Ferrari museum, and afterwards to dine at the famous Cavallino restaurant. And, who knows, should they happen to be dining there on a Sunday afternoon, they might be lucky enough to hear Maranello's church bells ringing out in celebration of the latest Formula 1 victory achieved by Ferrari's grand prix team. As a direct consequence of all of this, the very notion of Ferrari upping sticks and heading off elsewhere is beyond unthinkable. Maranello and Ferrari are quite indivisible, a single living entity.

Not only is this unbreakable connection extremely good for local commerce, it also adds exceptional strength to Ferrari's structure. The storied history of this long-legendary racing team lives and breaths within the tight confines of Maranello. Formula 1 drivers, engineers, aerodynamicists, and designers are drawn to this mystical location like nowhere else on earth; the town possesses a magical, beguiling lure. Ferrari is Maranello. Maranello is Ferrari.

I mention all of the above because this very special connection between Ferrari and Maranello – the tendril bond between the renowned racing team and the ancient fertile lands of the Emilia-Romagna valley – is the basis for the story you're about to read. I'm fascinated by the relentless passage of Time, how it inevitably affects everything in our world, yet, equally, how it seems to influence different things at different speeds: an olive tree appears to age far slower than does a man, for example. The local farmers of the hills and lands surrounding Maranello are forever being replaced, renewed generation by generation, while the olive trees they care for so tenderly remain solid and unmoved. A single mature olive tree will likely have felt the air of ten centuries diffusing through its branches. And a thousand-year-old tree understands the history of its homeland far better than we ever will, for Antiquity herself has whispered and shared firsthand her many stories with the listening leaves of her indulgent, faithful friend.

I've typeset the pages of this book as when I read the story to an audience: a 'live performance edition' printed with a fourteen-point Garamond font, and spaced paragraphs for ease of narration; the text itself divided into three distinct 'acts', this allowing for timed pauses throughout the reading; and it's my most sincere wish that you'll enjoy owning and reading *Always Ferrari* in this keepsake, souvenir format.

Steve Matchett.

ALWAYS FERRARI

“Nothing in this world is permanent, and we’re foolish when we ask anything to last, but surely we’re still more foolish not to take delight in it while we still have it.”

Somerset Maugham

PART ONE

THE TOLLING OF THE BELL - THE THOUSAND-YEAR-OLD OLIVE TREE - TIME WILL TELL - THE DAILY LIFE OF MARANELLO

[NARRATION – THIRTY MINUTES]

With no sense of achievement the yawning summer day had unexpectedly reached the hour of noon. The plodding morning seemed unconvinced that this had actually happened but eventually conceded that it must be true, for the bronze bell of Maranello's modest church tower had just tolled its twelve steady chimes across the sedimentary plains of the Emilia-Romagna valley. Up on the rolling hillside to the north of this small market town, a gnarled olive tree ruffled a sluggish response to the church bell's dutiful call, the tree's narrow leaves momentarily swirled by a brief, coiling breeze.

A blaze of white sun burned in the skies above the grove where this one particular olive tree had long ago pushed its twisting roots, and the smudges of heat haze rising from the dry farm tracks made the honey-coloured stone walls of the scattered hillside buildings shimmer with indistinct lines.

The surrounding meadows drowsed in the growing afternoon heat. Few creatures ventured from shade: burrowed rabbits stayed deep underground, and lethargic grasshoppers languidly chirruped to one another without enthusiasm, unwilling to move from their sheltered cover at the bottom of clumped grass; a safe haven where pale yellow stems held the last of the dawn's dew.

The striking of the midday bell signalled lunchtime in the town, a chance for sweating workers to lay down their tools, to eat and drink and to pause. Above all to pause. Life must not hurry during the hottest hours of an Italian summer, nothing good can come of it. The grasshoppers and rabbits are aware of this, albeit in a most simplistic way: their bodies reacting instinctively to the shifting heat of the day, a guiding sense insisting they ought remain shaded and still.

In contrast to these subconscious animal reflexes, the olive tree appreciates this knowledge on an entirely more elevated level. The olive tree is extremely old, and it has learned that a thorough understanding of anything in this world is only attained after many long years of personal experience. Enlightenment requires dedicated commitment, an unending process of quiet observance and devoted scholarship – and this one particular olive tree has experienced and quietly observed *hundreds* of these scorching Modena summers. And not only has it survived all these many summers, flourishing and growing stronger, it has also learned something new and revealing from each and every one of them.

In comparison to the fleeting lives of the transient creatures of the surrounding meadows, the olive tree has attained an immeasurable age; perhaps many more centuries of growth and learning stretch ahead of it. The tree does not know how long it will survive, beyond the predictable changing of the seasons it cannot foretell its own future, but its long experience of this hillside above Maranello has taught it an invaluable lesson: Life is measured in controlled beats, there is a natural rhythm to it all, everything is timed.

The olive tree knows all about Time. Sunrise to sunset, moonrise to moonset, the swirls of air diffusing through this quiet grove connect with the tree's green leaves. The wind and the olive tree enjoy a symbiotic relationship, one talks while the other listens.

Hour upon hour, the air currents of more than a thousand years have shared their tales with this olive tree: stories of terrible plagues; of empires rising and falling; of kings claiming ownership of immovable mountains, with newly drawn maps produced to bolster their nonsense claims. There are always stories of wars, of course: one global nightmare replacing another, an unending litany of utter stupidity, but occasionally the breeze carries fresh stories of growth and learning; green shoots of renaissance hope seen during fleeting periods of unnerving calm. The brief lulls between the wars, those necessary pauses to allow the canons to be repositioned; to allow the maps to be redrawn; to allow the troops to rearrange themselves; to allow new allegiances to be signed, and new betrayals to be seeded in fertile ground.

Of all the world's creatures to visit this hillside grove, only man seems intent on rushing his allotted time. Not a single day unfolds without these misguided beasts yearning for their next meaningless disagreement, most trying to claim ownership of concepts quite beyond their limited understanding, a species of life permanently distracted from any hope of unity by their preoccupation of devising ever more terrible ways of obliterating one another. Folly.

And only mankind acts in this irrational way. Other visitors to the olive grove merely live in the moment: the grasshoppers and the rabbits, the goats, the sheep and the cattle, all of these and many other animals besides, all of them merely experience the grove in the time they are given; changing nothing, destroying nothing, killing only to live and dying only when it is their correct time to die.

The olive tree knows mankind to be the one irrational exception to this otherwise universal philosophy. The olive tree does not understand why this should be but it is certainly true, nonetheless for that, something it has seen endlessly repeated for more than ten centuries. Even after all these long years, however, even given mankind's self-destructive nature, his predisposition for reckless chaos, the olive tree makes no judgement of these unknowable beings. It would do no good, there is no arboreal defence against the might of a swinging axe, so judging mankind for his unfathomable acts of hostility would serve no purpose. Instead, the olive tree's adopted approach is simply one of *living*: to peacefully coexist, to observe the daily happenings in the grove and, for as long as Time allows, to silently ponder the wind's latest stories.

There are many similar wizened old olive trees in this ancient grove, and over the centuries many hundreds of sharp blades have carved all manner of runes and dates and symbols into their deep, hardened trunks. But on this one particular tree – the one gnarled olive tree that just now ruffled its dusty leaves in response to Maranello's church bell tolling the hour of noon – picked out in a series of deeply scarred letters, there is but one word: *Sempre.*

***

Sitting in the un-mown grass of the grove, my back resting against the gnarled trunk of this olive tree, I gazed down into the valley below through my old shabby field glasses, elbows held tight against my knees to better support my arms. Ignoring the pits and scratches of the aged lenses, I work the focus wheel until a kaleidoscope of blurs and smudges gradually sharpen to form a group of weathered stone buildings: farmhouses and barns built with meter-thick walls designed to last forever; understated masterpieces of solidity patiently erected by itinerant field workers in dormant, long gone winter months.

Another two turns of the adjustment wheel extend the binoculars' focal range to its maximum, revealing more distant details, images of the town centre itself. A squat two-story factory, reddish brown in colour, showed through the lenses; the brick walls of this building clearly decades newer than those of the sentinel farmhouses on the town's outskirts.

Small groups of exiting workers crisscross the quiet road adjacent the factory's modest entrance. Leaving via a guarded gateway, some of them cross this road on the faded lines of a painted pedestrian crossing, while others seem eager to pause a while, lighting a lunchtime cigarette before moving on.

Beyond this roadside entrance, a simple oblong service tunnel penetrates the factory's exterior walls, providing its workers with access to an invisible inner sanctum. The factory's colourful exterior is there for all to see and enjoy but any additional buildings, those built beyond the factory's unassuming (though guarded) archway remain hidden from view.

With its neatly painted façade, its secure access tunnel and concealed inner layout, the overall impression is one of a loyally protected stronghold, a private bastion built right in the heart of Maranello. Above this particular building's entrance, clearly marked in distinctive yellow letters on its smooth *terra di Siena* painted walls, there is but one word: *Ferrari.*

***

Housed on the other side of the rectangular service tunnel, and extending far beyond the quaint frontage of the original factory building sits the contemporary state-of-the-art multi-billion-dollar manufacturing facility for Enzo Ferrari's world-famous motor cars. Enzo moved his headquarters to Maranello in 1943, the midst of the second world war, and although German forces were fast retreating by this stage, hastily leaving Italy via its northern borders, his factory was hit and damaged by allied bombing. The brickwork was repaired, however, and his engineering work there continued, with Enzo Ferrari producing his first road car in 1947. And the rest, as they say, is history.

Over the years, as demand for Enzo's exquisite machines continued to increase, so did the inevitable piecemeal additions to his production plant. Growth was necessary, and I assume it would have been a relatively easy ask for Ferrari's ranked lawyers to have sought planning permission from Modena's civic authorities to demolish and sweep aside their original brick factory, to replace all that once was with a glittering new design, some futuristic structure housing everything from molten foundry work to the pristine stitching of Connolly leather upholstery; the entire dream car manufacturing process contained under a single, sterile roof.

Mercifully, however, nothing could be further from Ferrari's philosophy. For this one particular car manufacturer, the one housed within this gracefully preserved building sitting in the heart of a sleepy Italian market town, Tradition is of paramount importance.

***

I lowered my binoculars, the nape of my neck tingling with excitement. The sight of those immovable stone farmhouses, the sense of history they carried, this along with the wonderful views of Ferrari's handsome factory, it was all quite captivating. No, captivating isn't enough, the images seen through my old field glasses had generated an altogether more powerful emotion: these images were truly *enchanting.*

I delicately stowed my binoculars in their frail brown leather case, wiping clean the contours of the lenses with tender care. These field glasses were given to me, a most treasured gift from a most treasured friend. They are now more than a hundred years old, and their increasingly fragile case needs a light touch. The stitching of the lid's leather hinge has grown worryingly weak over the years, much of its aged threading has now frayed away but it still works, dutifully holding the binoculars safe inside.

This lazy summer morning in Italy had passed all too easily. Sitting here, enjoying the solitude of this forgotten olive grove, pondering the past, and recalling similar long summer days in England, the days of my childhood. Life never sits still for long... though sometimes I wish it did.

I thought of my precious field glasses and of those magnified images of the reddish brick factory in the town below the hillside. The Ferrari factory is something very special, and seeing it through these cherished binoculars has elated me, filling me with happiness. And in this special moment I'm suddenly aware of having fulfilled a promise to a long-departed friend.

***

This abandoned olive grove has created a wonderful feeling of nostalgia for me. I'm reluctant to leave but I cannot spend all day leaning against this gnarled tree, it's time to make a move. "Onward and upward," as my dad would have said, and with more than a little hesitancy I gingerly regained my feet: an all too familiar twinge from my lower back reminding me of its unwillingness to help.

The heat of the afternoon is growing fierce. I took a long pull of San Pellegrino, the sharp bubbles popping in my mouth as I eagerly swallowed the water. Packing away the remains of my unfinished picnic, I scattered a handful of cured black olives and tiny sweet tomatoes in the grass for the rabbits to find, when the coolness of the evening urges them to snuffle the air. The ancient olive tree watched me as I wandered off to find my car. I had been merely one more uninvited visitor to its private domain. I had arrived, I had rested and now I was leaving, all without saying a word of please or thank you. The olive tree watched me go but it appeared not to judge me, despite my trespassing on its land.

Seemingly in cahoots with my lower back, my equally complaining 1939 Citroën was also proving persistently stubborn and unwilling to help. The fuel in her carburettor had boiled away. I had half expected this would happen (we've come to know one another reasonably well over the years) and I'd hoped that leaving her to snooze under the spreading branches of a nearby chestnut tree, although admittedly meagre shade, might help in keeping her cool. Evidently, however, this had not kept her cool in any way whatsoever. The car's engine bay had steadily grown seething hot; this, in turn, evaporating the petrol sitting in the carb's float chamber.

I knew what was needed, a relatively simple cure; two minutes later I had the air filter removed and was patiently dabbing the carb's housing, its float chamber and connecting fuel line with a cloth doused in the last of the San Pellegrino. I bathed her like this for a while, eventually fanning her dry with a folded copy of *The Telegraph* newspaper, gradually reducing her temperature while at the same time reassuring her that everything would be absolutely fine, that she mustn't worry about a thing. I suspect mechanics and nurses have much in common.

This compassionate display of loving care was then followed by some distinctly uncompassionate curse words as I enthusiastically worked the starter motor, cranking and eventually coaxing all four engine cylinders to wake up and pay attention. Tough love, they call this part of the treatment. It worked, it always works. Ten minutes later my *Traction Avant* and I are firm friends once again, the pair of us weaving through the deserted back roads of Maranello in search of the Planet hotel, with the narrow tyres of my adorable (if strangely neurotic) old Citroën humming a happy song as we merrily drive along the town's sticky tarmac.

INTERMISSION

PART TWO

THE CAVALLINO - ALWAYS FERRARI - THE MONTANA - SCUDERIA FERRARI - A SHORT DRIVE TO A GOOD DINNER

[NARRATION – THIRTY-SIX MINUTES]

There are two restaurants in Maranello with notable associations with Scuderia Ferrari, the esteemed racing department of the parent company, the men and women responsible for its Formula 1 operations. The restaurant closest to the factory, *Ristorante Cavallino*, is located, quite literally, across the narrow street from Ferrari's gates. Anyone with but a passing interest in Ferrari's storied history will be aware of the Cavallino. This yellow stuccoed building is something of big deal in this small town; Enzo Ferrari himself regularly dined here, its interior walls continue to host myriad aging photographs, their captured smiles recalling just how jolly these lengthy meals used to be.

Dear old Enzo, *il Commendatore* or *il grande vecchio* – the great old man, as he was known in his autumn years – lived a full and clearly very productive life. He died in the summer of 1988, aged ninety, right here in Maranello. A local man from birth to death. On his quiet leaving of this world, his name and the fame of his business empire was already known throughout its four most distant corners.

It's been some years since this most celebrated of customers took his final lunchtime stroll across the road in front of his brick factory, to eat a little fresh pasta in the cooled interior of the Cavallino but, nevertheless, Enzo's former hangout remains a popular destination for countless numbers of devoted Maranello tourists. There remains no shortfall of eager customers longing to share stories with their excited friends back home of when they, too, enjoyed a memorable dish of virgin-oiled spaghetti and a glass of fine Barolo in this iconic local restaurant. And why not? I'm sure there are also those affected few who delight in telling friends that they *may* have dined in the Cavallino when last they toured Italy, but they simply can't recall the event, life being such a dizzying whirl of social engagements, *"…honestly, darlings, who can remember these things?"* Oh, make no mistake, they can remember right enough.

The Cavallino's story is a part of Ferrari's story, of that there is no doubt, and the restaurant continues to make best use of its past association with its most famous former customer. Seen in this light, perhaps the Cavallino is similar to Harry's Bar in Venice, the erstwhile haunt of Ernest Hemingway, Orson Welles and Charlie Chaplin: its past clientele assures its present clientele? For myself, I have experienced just one evening inside the walls of the Cavallino, and most certainly it was the restaurant's connection to Enzo Ferrari that took me there.

The occasion was a small festive dinner on a bitterly cold evening, back in 2009. Earlier that same day, before visiting the Cavallino, four colleagues and I had completed a substantial film shoot inside Ferrari's factory. Commissioned by Speed Channel, an American television network, the project involved two lengthy days of on-camera work, during which we interviewed several key players including Chris Vlahos, the director of their classic road car restoration division, Andrea Galletti, the director of their classic race car restoration division, and Stefano Domenicali, team principal of the famed Scuderia Ferrari.

Both Chris Vlahos and Stefano Domenicali were charmingly obliging, patiently waiting to be interviewed while my producer and his cameramen played with backdrops and lighting and various camera settings to achieve the best possible shots. All of this painstaking preparation is unavoidably time consuming, but this initial attention to detail pays dividends later on, lending an elegant polish to the finished, edited production.

Along with his two colleagues, Andrea Galletti had also gone above and beyond to ensure our show was a success. Back in the 1990s Andrea worked as a race engineer with Scuderia Ferrari. I remembered him from our mutual time in the F1 paddock, and we were soon chatting and laughing about the good old days, recounting tales of when we both pounded around the world together, endlessly dashing from country to country, from one Formula 1 race track to another. As the old adage says: you can take the mechanics out of the pit lane but you can never take the pit lane out of the mechanics.

More doors continued to open for us, and we were given the opportunity to interview Ferrari's current grand prix drivers, Filipe Massa and Kimi Raikkonen. Filipe proved an absolute pleasure to work with, I cannot overstate his willingness to assist with our filming. The twenty-eight-year-old driver smiled easily, naturally, engaging the camera and giving measured thought to my questions before responding; his answers were considered, and yet open and unguarded.

Filipe showed himself to be a true professional throughout the entire interview process. This is a man who fully embraces his role with Maranello, understanding his commitments to Ferrari both *in* and *out* of a race car. Contemporary motor sport is a mammoth commercial business, and the industry of grand prix racing places unending demands on its drivers; the media wants to interview them, the world wants to see them. It can be a tedious slog, I understand that, but in Filipe's case I gained no impression that today's filming was merely another contractual obligation, simply one more promotional commitment to be endured in order to appease his paymasters. Not a bit of it, for Filipe's eyes glowed with genuine affection as he talked of his life with Ferrari, describing exactly how special it all is, often referring to his colleagues, the team's ranks of mechanics and engineers as his family. Talking with me that day, looking directly into our camera, he willingly shared with our viewers his deep-rooted passion for this ultra-famous company, and his delight in being in such hallowed surroundings was just as self-evident, even when our cameras were not rolling.

We shook hands at the end of our time together, a firm handshake with eye contact: an authentic gesture, and my lasting impression will always be that of meeting a refreshingly honest man, sincere in his approach to life: a successful yet humble Formula 1 driver who genuinely *loves* Ferrari. This emotion is impossible to fake. Our eyes truly are windows to the soul.

***

The completed thirty-minute program, *Always Ferrari*, aired on Speed Channel a few weeks later, broadcast coast-to-coast across America. Thankfully, our audience looked on it most kindly; my employers sufficiently pleased as to allow me to continue working with them... a welcome reward in and of itself.

And that little festive dinner in the Cavallino, (my one visit there, mentioned earlier), this would represent our production crew's modest wrap party: a meal celebrating the end of our shoot. In using that rather glitzy expression, *wrap party*, I've likely made our late evening supper sound unavoidably more Hollywood than it actually was… but wrap party is (I'm reliably informed) the correct vernacular. You'll appreciate, however, that I deliberately reined back from saying 'end of principal photography wrap party' which would certainly have overdone the thing. I'm reasonably certain that our Maranello dining experience was notably more subdued than any movie-biz wrap party celebrated in the swanky nightspots of Beverly Hills.

PART TWO

The windswept plazas of Maranello were conspicuously deserted when our merry band headed out of our hotel for the brief, slippery walk to the Cavallino: A bitter midweek night in the midst of a deep midwinter generates little enthusiasm in the locals to venture out and socialise in the town's plethora of bars and cafés; Maranello's wise inhabitants choosing to forego the treachery of icy pavements, preferring instead to stay home, warming their toes by a crackling fire while watching game shows on the television.

I do not blame them for staying indoors, although the unavoidable consequence of their decision was that the majority of the Cavallino's linen-draped tables would remain immaculately unsullied that night, spotless and ready for the following day's lunch service. And, sure enough, upon our arrival in the famed restaurant the place was indeed conspicuously quiet, devoid of any noticeable clank of pots and pans coming from within their kitchen, something I always find rather cheery. Also, there was an equally noticeable absence of any music. No songs (be them romantic or jolly in tempo) dared to disturb the cloistral stillness of the silent interior.

Nevertheless, standing together within a small reception area, we were cordially greeted, then gracefully guided into the legendary dining room. The waiters assigned to take care of us were all extremely polite. Two of them willingly seated our group, noted our orders and dutifully served us, as is their want. And there they left us, all alone in the spacious calm of their grand *sala da pranzo*, its unlit corners impenetrable to the eye. The food was *exceedingly* good. We talked in hushed tones during dinner, by far the louder sounds were those of our knives and forks clinking on china plates.

Further into the evening, now replete and feeling a little sleepy, our dishes were cleared away and we were again left entirely undisturbed. Sufficiently uninterrupted, in fact, for us to extend quite serious consideration to the question of alienation with regards the human condition, with this rather lengthy discourse transitioning to an exchange of views on the theme of mortality in general and the tragically fragile nature of our own brief existence. And beyond the *sotto* notes of our own suitably muted dialogue, the pressing stillness of the Cavallino's elegant interior remained perfectly inviolate.

When eventually our waiter returned to address our needs, we as an assembly decided against the taking of desserts and coffee. Our faces fixed with wan expressions we told how we had become aware of the impermanence of life, and that there remained much we still needed to do in the decreasingly short time available to us. One of our group said he would telephone his mother first thing in the morning to make amends for past failings, (his own mother, you understand, not the waiter's) but for now we must simply move on, stand up and walk away.

Our waiter pressed a reassuringly full-bodied bill of services atop the table's crisp white linen, and we did all that was expected of us before sloping away, out into the starlit brilliance of a frosty night; with this rather chilly exit concluding my one and only visit to the famed *Ristorante Cavallino.* Our evening there was most memorable, no question about that, and (should ever the opportunity present itself) I would waste no time in dining there again.

My personal wintery experience notwithstanding, given more clement weather, days when banks of greying snows do not line the town's narrow roads, I'm sure the Cavallino has no problem in filling its many handsome tables. With its long-established connections to Ferrari's past leadership, the restaurant remains an enduring legend. And long may that legend endure, for through its willingness to entertain Maranello's many excited summer visitors, the Cavallino provides a much-appreciated service to the contemporary employees of Scuderia Ferrari, those passionate designers, engineers and mechanics of the present era, all toiling to secure Ferrari's future success.

***

The burden placed on Ferrari's Formula 1 racing staff is truly immense. As a team, they are charged with but one task: To win. To win everything there is to win. A herculean task for any group, given the difficulty of the technical challenges and the relentless psychological stresses imposed by this intense form of competition. In Ferrari's own case, however, it is all but impossible for their present personnel to better the triumphs of their forbears.

From the early days of those original grainy F1 races of the 1950s until today, this company's racing department has amassed a truly phenomenal series of international sporting records. Scuderia Ferrari have secured more pole positions, set more fastest laps, scored more points, won more races, and claimed more Formula 1 world championships (both constructors' and drivers' titles) than any other team in the long, distinguished history of the sport.

Naturally, some seasons have been more fruitful than others, some race cars (and some drivers) have proven stronger than others. The very nature of F1 competition means all grand prix teams will experience periods of feast and famine: At this level of engineering excellence, with its requirement for extreme high-performance machinery (and therefore its unavoidable delicate fragility) mercurial success is inevitable and – to a limited degree – is accepted as an element of the challenge. That said, in seeking a holistic evaluation of Ferrari's grand prix campaigns, the Formula 1 history books recount a most compelling story of this legendary team's remarkable accomplishments.

Given the length of Ferrari's involvement in this sport, it stands to reason that not all of these record-setting results have been secured through the efforts of the same dedicated personnel. As with any company, Ferrari's prestigious roster is always subject to change: team presidents and principals, sporting and technical directors, chief designers and aerodynamicists, engineers and mechanics, machinists and composite workers, race drivers, too; any individual position within any given department of Maranello is as impermanent as life itself.

Similar to the renewal of cells within a living body, each grand prix specialist (at one time passionately attracted by the allure of working for this famed organisation) will be replaced. This is a certainty, a perfectly natural state of affairs. Over a period of time, worker by worker, Ferrari's *entire* payroll will be completely rejuvenated. This has already happened many times over.

The individual cells of the body are different, but Ferrari as a concept remains unaltered, a fixed, immovable entity. By embracing this process of regeneration Ferrari and its public identity, its *rosso corsa* race cars, its famous 'prancing horse' emblem, its modest brick factory, its storied history, all of these things are cast permanent. In this way Scuderia Ferrari is similar to the ancient olive tree perched on the hillside above Maranello: over the centuries countless farmers have nurtured and protected it with devoted loving care; individually the farmers are impermanent – mortal beings live brief lives – but from generation to generation their skills are handed on, their combined knowledge survives. And the tended olive tree itself outlasts them all.

***

Given the Scuderia's remarkable past achievements, the unending challenge for their race team of tomorrow is simply to keep on winning, to continually grow these staggering numbers and, arguably of greater importance, to *never* allow one of their precious hard-earned records to fall into the grasping hands of an upcoming rival.

***

I mentioned earlier that there are *two* Maranello restaurants with strong associations to Ferrari. The first we have discussed, the other is *Ristorante Montana*. Don't worry if the name is new to you, there is a very good reason why it may have escaped your attention: it is an *extremely* popular restaurant with the employees of the Scuderia. On any given day, lunchtime or evening this little tucked-away eatery is likely bustling with Formula 1 mechanics, engineers and designers, grand prix drivers, too, when they are in town. The majority of those who eat here would prefer to be left in peace; the Montana is a sanctuary, a quiet haven away from the relentless pressures within Ferrari's factory. I'm not suggesting the restaurant's location is a closely guarded secret (for a cursory Google search will swiftly reveal its coordinates) but the address of the Montana tends not to be telegraphed by those who relish its intimacy.

Eighteen-hour days are nothing unusual for Scuderia Ferrari's dedicated staff, and the Montana provides them temporary refuge: a calm and soothing respite from flickering computer screens and the intricate assembly work of moulded carbon and machined titanium. Inside the Montana's smooth wooden doors, a corner table awaits, its round top covered with simple unpretentious cloth. The restaurant's interior is softly lit by a relaxing diffused glow: a warm and inviting ambiance allowing tired eyes to rest.

Phones are set to silence within these walls, just for a while. It is time to pause Maranello's working day, time to allow the Montana's discreet staff to serve crisp green salads drizzled in local olive oils. After this initial refreshment comes homemade pasta, pulled *al dente* firm from the pot, stoic enough to support strong regional sauces fortified with ripped herbs and crushed garlic; everything carefully simmered to a reduced, softly bubbling perfection. Then there are steaming soups and sizzling roast meats, crunchy roast potatoes, aged parmesan cheeses and fragrant tiramisu.

These much-desired things are the mouth-watering comfort foods of Modena, and this family run restaurant knows them all inside out. From their intimate knowledge of these inherited northern Italian recipes, to the hunting of the perfect local ingredients needed to prepare them authentically, to the peaceful dining room service itself, every aspect of this modest restaurant's daily routine carries an unforced rhythm; as natural a process as the nearby hillside trees working to produce their precious seasonal crop of oiled fruit.

The staff's warm welcome is always spontaneous and genuine, and whenever I dine here I enjoy the idea that the *Ristorante Montana* represents a direct connection to Italy's historic past: from the time of those earliest olive farmers until today, this unassuming delight of a place is the very living heritage of those remarkable hardworking farming families of the ancient Emilia-Romagna valley.

As for the restaurant's hungry regulars visiting from that famed squat two-story factory down the road, a restful three courses here (complete with a parting shot of robust espresso) provide these overworked engineers with sufficient drive to give another productive eight hours of themselves once back within Ferrari's guarded fortress.

PART TWO

***

Thankfully, the air has cooled to something approaching comfortable by eight o'clock in the evening, and my old Citroën fired into life without need of medical attention. The drive from the Planet to the Montana takes less than five minutes: merely exit the hotel's garage, drive past Ferrari's gateway on the right, on past *Via Tazio Nuvolari*, which is also on the right; then the Fiorano track, over on the left. Continue on (over the little bridge on the outskirts of town) and here take the first left, this doubling back along a secluded service road. And there stands the Montana.

Far from a complex journey, and for such a brief excursion it may seem unnecessary to drive. On a warm, still evening such as tonight, if heading to restaurants in the opposite direction, those located around the town's church, the centre of Maranello, then a gentle stroll would be most inviting, romantic even, given the right company but, alas, the roads stretching away to the north of Ferrari's gates, the town's outskirts, these routes are not kind to the wants of pedestrians.

My arrival in the Montana is met with a welcoming smile, a beckoned invite to a quiet spot in the rear of their dining room, a table where the unobtrusive notes of violins blend easily with the low purr of diffused conversation. The place is already busy, but the atmosphere is far from hurried. The restaurant's waiters remain at ease, measured, still able to chat placidly with their customers, pausing to share in an exchange or to tell a brief story while serving their wines and breads and salads and roasted meats. The ambience of the dining room is warm and casual, and my supper promises to be a wonderful conclusion to what has already been a near perfect day.

INTERMISSION

PART THREE

NIGEL STEPNEY - THREE AMBITIONS - TEARS OF THE STRONG - THE TOLLING OF THE BELL - A FAREWELL TO ARMS

[NARRATION – THIRTY MINUTES]

My dining companion, Nigel Stepney, Scuderia Ferrari's chief mechanic joined me five minutes later. Nigel used to be Benetton's chief mechanic; back in 1990 it was Nigel who gave me my big break, employing me in the role of race mechanic, working alongside him on Benetton's Formula 1 team. I owe him a considerable debt of gratitude for this life-changing act of selfless charity.

Much to my immense relief, my first conversation with Nigel (during that long-ago face-to-face interview) revolved around all things Ferrari. I had no Formula 1 credentials but I had extensive experience of servicing and restoring classic Ferrari road cars, knowledge diligently gained throughout my career to this watershed moment, and Nigel seemed fascinated by all of the meticulous assembly work, the precision detail which these multi-million dollar sports cars demanded.

Thankfully, Benetton's chief mechanic appreciated all I could tell him, evidently intrigued to hear of Maranello's intricate procedures for casting an authentic replacement engine cylinder block for a sports car of the 1960s, with the factory's mechanics ensuring that this freshly cast block carries the correct serial numbers to identify this engine as truly being the next in the production run of a particular series of engines, even if there had been a lengthy sabbatical, perhaps a break of many years in that production run.

I could see in Nigel's eyes how drawn he was to all of this, a man naturally empathic with this detailed engineering work, the fastidious accuracy of Maranello's documentation, the dedication and commitment necessary to maintain this degree of excellence.

***

In later months, now working alongside Nigel Stepney during our Benetton days, I soon discovered that all three of these facets: devoted commitment, detailed record-keeping, and unremitting accuracy were the three stamped hallmarks of his highly respected methodology.

Nigel made things happen. He made a difference, never settling for anything less than perfection in all things. Arguably, as a consequence of this he was *never* an easy man to work with; notorious for expecting his staff to give *everything* of themselves (with sleep a rare luxury during race weekends) but he *always* led by example: Early morning or late night, Nigel Stepney was either in his office or working directly on the race cars. He lived to make a difference, to always improve: Any tiny component, any small procedure, *anything* and *everything* was continually honed in order to make the cars in his charge faster and more reliable; the mechanics in his charge swifter and more efficient.

***

During that initial interview with Nigel, just as he had found my background with Ferrari's road cars to be of interest, I was equally drawn to Nigel's own experiences, his considerable Formula 1 knowledge, his evident passion to succeed in this demanding, exhausting industry. Chatting with him that day, I found his obvious love of grand prix racing, his willingness to give his all (to better his chances of winning the F1 constructors' world championship) to be deeply profound.

The two of us had discovered common ground: our mutual admiration for the craftsmanship of Maranello's products; our combined respect for the achievements of this famous racing team. Consequently, my Benetton interview seemed effortless, and to a degree (even given the formal context of our conversation) Nigel and I definitely bonded that day, the pair of us exchanging our respective stories: me describing the famous Colombo 250 V12s, Nigel praising the beautifully clean lines of John Barnard's 1989 640 F1 chassis.

That said, even given our relaxed dialogue that day, I never guessed just how appealing a potential career with Ferrari was to Nigel's ambitions. Over the following years, however, throughout our many subsequent conversations, Nigel eventually confided in me, telling me of his three career objectives: To work with Ayrton Senna. To work with Scuderia Ferrari. To win world championships with Ayrton Senna, with the pair of them working together in Maranello.

Lofty aspirations for anyone to contemplate, but Nigel Stepney knew *exactly* what he wanted to accomplish. Moreover, he had already achieved one of these three desired things: securing the role as 'number one' mechanic on Ayrton Senna's race car during their mutual time together with Lotus, this back in the mid-nineteen-eighties. And with Nigel having worked so closely with Ayrton, observing this young Brazilian's talents openly flourish, I'm sure all of this remarkable experience only helped to sow the seeds of Nigel's other two career ambitions.

Senna quit Lotus at the conclusion of 1987, this marking his momentous move to McLaren International, with Ron Dennis offering Ayrton an unmissable opportunity to drive alongside Alain Prost. The tales of Prost and Senna's phenomenal series of drives and duels throughout 1988 have become the stuff of motor racing legend. With McLaren winning fifteen of sixteen races, their team's Honda-powered cars finished the year just one victory shy of a perfect, unbeaten season. Only Ferrari prevented this from happening, they scoring a remarkable one-two finish in their home grand prix, in Monza, although, quite frankly, even this was more a result of both McLarens failing to finish, as opposed to any direct challenge from Maranello's forces.

There's no question, Ayrton Senna's move to McLaren provided Nigel Stepney with all the impetus he needed to forge ahead, to improve his own standing within this industry. Leaving Lotus and moving to Oxfordshire, he accepted a significant career promotion, joining Benetton Formula Ltd. as their new chief mechanic.

Benetton's latest signing would not remain settled for long, however, and by the January of 1993 (in Senna's final year with McLaren) Nigel made yet another remarkable move, this one a genuine astonishment to many: this time appointed chief mechanic to Scuderia Ferrari, the first English chief mechanic employed by Ferrari throughout this famous marque's long history. And with this relocation to Maranello, Nigel had now achieved *two* of his three career ambitions.

Alas, his third would never be possible.

Nigel was always a strong man, not merely physically but also emotionally: eternally stoic, resilient under immense pressure. Never one to reveal his private feelings, the only time I saw him openly distraught, unabashedly wiping tears from his eyes was on the afternoon of May 1st 1994, in Imola, Italy, on his hearing confirmation of the tragic news of Ayrton's fatal accident during the San Marino grand prix. I found Nigel in this raw state directly after this thoroughly ghastly race had finally ended. Standing alone in the Imola pit lane he seemed completely destroyed. He looked defenceless and utterly vulnerable but as I moved forward, wanting to console him in some unknown way, he swiftly turned, backing away from me, disappearing within the darkened depths of Ferrari's pit garage; a man both desolate and entirely inconsolable.

***

We will never know if Ayrton Senna would ever have driven for Ferrari, or if that potential partnership would have blossomed and succeeded in securing more race wins and more world championships. My understanding is that Ayrton had, indeed, signed a 'letter of intent', a rather informal agreement of mutual interest between both parties, this perhaps leading to preliminary contract negotiations – although I'm unaware of any firm dates having been agreed for these opening talks, nor do I know of any additional (more binding) documents having been inked.

None of that really matters, I suppose. Not in any objective way, simply the Senna/Ferrari partnership never happened. That said, I do enjoy the tantalising idea of Ayrton and Ferrari working together, the daydream that Ayrton would one day have walked through that iconic Maranello gateway to begin the scintillating Ferrari chapter of his illustrious career. I imagine it a truly exciting partnership; thrilling to see that famous yellow helmet resolutely bobbing around inside a *rosso corsa* race car built by the skilled mechanics of Scuderia Ferrari.

I like to close my eyes, to escape reality for a moment, there to see a smiling Ayrton Senna climbing from his Ferrari, accepting and holding aloft the silver trophy from Monza. Ayrton Senna: winner of the Italian grand prix, a sparkling trophy held high in both hands, all to the resounding roaring cheers of the thousands of gathered *tifosi*, the packed race track below the podium a swirling ocean of scarlet red: *"Senna! Senna! Senna!"*

***

Although fate had decreed that Nigel and Ayrton could never again work together, Nigel opted to remain with Ferrari, eventually receiving the prestigious rank of Race Technical Manager. And come the close of 1995, when Michael Schumacher made his own momentous move from Benetton to Ferrari, Nigel played an integral role in helping to secure a phenomenal series of Maranello victories, a string of race wins culminating in *five* consecutive drivers' titles... and *six* consecutive constructors' titles. Those six magical years, 1999 to 2004, will likely always be known as the most incredible years of unbridled success in the long life of the black prancing horse. And Nigel Stepney was right there to witness every magical moment.

Throughout the majority of Michael Schumacher's tenure, the efficiency of Ferrari's race team went unmatched. The Scuderia's mechanics were swift and well drilled in the pit stops, and the build quality and reliability of their complex race cars was the envy of the entire F1 paddock. Much of this proficiency was a result of Nigel's own uncompromising standards: his unforgiving attention to detail in all things, his pre-race preparations and his unending commitment to be the best in the industry, his relentless *desire* to win.

***

I eventually departed Benetton in 1998, leaving Oxford's dreaming spires in favour of a pastoral corner of western France, a hamlet of solitude, a place to pursue my fledgling writing career. A fresh start and a new chapter for me, but I didn't abandon my former pit lane colleagues altogether, staying in touch with Nigel Stepney via telephone and email. Understandably, our correspondence was often sporadic; for although the pace of my own life had suddenly slowed, Nigel's remained *exceedingly* busy (working for Ferrari does this without even trying) but I knew he would always offer assistance, should ever the need arise.

Tapping away on the text of an intended grand prix trilogy, I also welcomed any proffered freelance assignments, periodic work which helped to pay for my firewood, this and many miscellaneous parts for a wheezing antique Citroën. In the May of 2000, *The Telegraph*, an English broadsheet kindly commissioned me to write a story on Maranello's chief mechanic, with the newspaper's editor asking me to flesh out something of Nigel's duties, his daily responsibilities within the team's ever evolving structure.

Considering Ferrari's recent run of success, the paper's commission was especially timely: their race team having just returned the coveted F1 constructors' trophy back to Maranello; the first time they had managed this feat in sixteen long years. Moreover, with both Michael Schumacher and Ferrari now in strident form, the partnership looked set to win *both* prestigious titles: the drivers' world championship and the constructors' world championship by the close of 2000.

Ferrari's outstanding resurgence made for compelling storytelling, and Nigel's own story, his part in all of this, was one simply asking to be written. I swiftly accepted the editor's offer, and a midnight telephone conversation with Nigel supplied me with all the essential quotes needed to give the piece its credibility. The late hour of this call was at Nigel's own request, a time when even the hectic workload within the halls of Maranello tends to slow to a more manageable pace.

PART THREE

The Telegraph seemed delighted with my filed story, and the only request made by Nigel was to receive a copy of the newspaper. Longing for any excuse to take my now semi-restored *Traction Avant* for a leisurely spin across the valleys of France and down into dips and hills of Italy, I readily promised to deliver his newspaper by hand.

***

With no sense of achievement the yawning summer day had unexpectedly reached the hour of noon. The plodding morning seemed unconvinced that this had actually happened but eventually conceded that it must be true, for the bronze bell of Maranello's modest church tower had just tolled its twelve steady chimes across the sedimentary plains of the Emilia-Romagna valley. Up on the rolling hillside to the north of this small market town, a gnarled olive tree ruffled a sluggish response to the church bell's dutiful call, the tree's narrow leaves momentarily swirled by a brief, coiling breeze.

Driving away from Maranello, heading back towards France on the morning after my dinner with Nigel, with my old Citroën now trundling past a squat factory built with *terra di Siena* painted walls, I couldn't see the ancient olive tree up in its hillside grove... but I knew it was there, silently listening to the wind's latest stories. Each day is a new day, and for a thousand years this one particular olive tree has studied the ever-changing faces of those who live and work in this ancient valley.

***

Nigel Stepney died on May 2nd 2014. He died in a traffic accident in the early hours of the morning following the twentieth anniversary remembrances of Ayrton Senna's own death. For reasons unexplained, Nigel had parked his vehicle on the side of a motorway in England, he had then walked into the carriageway, and was there hit by an articulated goods vehicle. He was pronounced dead at the scene.

Nigel was not a perfect man but, then again, I know none who are. In our time working together with Benetton I got to know but a fraction of the man himself. Certainly, we respected one another; I admired his work with Ferrari, and he was always supportive of my writing. Throughout the years we always remained on friendly terms, yet I hesitate to call us genuine friends... for I was never allowed to get that close. Nigel didn't want that.

Our correspondence remained sporadic, but over time it became increasingly unusual for me to hear from him. Around a month before he died, however, Nigel called my cell phone, quite out of the blue. I remember, I was on a *TGV* train at the time, whistling along the high-speed tracks to Paris, from there boarding a flight to New York. We chatted for a few minutes, the call concerning nothing in particular, but before hanging up he paused a moment, asking if I was happy. I told him I was, I was enjoying life, my new role in the sport as a television broadcaster. Nigel told me he was pleased to hear it. “I’m pleased to hear that,” he said, and I knew he meant it.

***

There are many stories concerning Nigel Stepney, but this is the one I wanted to share.

THE END

ABOUT THE AUTHOR

STEVE MATCHETT

Steve Matchett played an intrinsic role in securing all three of Benetton's Formula 1 world championships.

He has written several books to date, of which *The Mechanic's Tale* continues to hold an Orion house record: their all-time best-selling motor racing title.

For the past twenty years he has worked as a television broadcaster with American networks NBC and FOX. He also works as a voiceover artist, a narrator of audiobooks.

The author hosts two online domains:
SteveMatchett.com & TheseDesiredThings.com

Made in the USA
Coppell, TX
20 August 2022